Quest For Ions

Quest For Ions
Poetry Collection 2011-2021

First published in 2021 by Poiesis Publishers (UK)

Cover artwork and design by Olya Dyer
Cover photograph by Browzan

ISBN 978-1-5272-9638-1

Quest For Ions

by

Browzan

2021

Contents

Preface by Christopher Brown

It took me years to accept
that I was an artist.
But here I am,
laid bare before you:
an image from the future.

Why do we make art?
For me,
it's a deeply personal exploration -
a dialogue with myself -
to generate an index of life and
connect with people.

Do artists fear extinction?
Is an artwork an attempt to defeat death?
Unconsciously,
this may be true of every endeavour -
the first rule of nature
is to survive.

Creativity is a way of life;
can't live with it,
can't live without it.

For all you misfits out there,
mad enough
to walk the tightrope
of self-expression,
hear this now:
I commend your courage!
Within this
mesmerising undertaking,
you'll be confronted by
myriad moments of
deepening despair,
but as long as
you never give up,
call upon
your inner strength
in times of strife,
then you will
have paid the ultimate price
for freedom:
living life
on your own terms.
If anyone mocks you,
for staying true
to your
raison d'etre.

Remember:

you are not
who others say
you are,
you are
who you
choose to be.

The meaning of your life
is something you create.

Noam Chomsky

Page one

In the starry night
your radiance
swirls
like the murmuration
of sea-beamed
pearls.

Peace

I see an ocean,
cyan
clear
humble waves
glide with
perfect sand
palm trees
dance in the gentle wind
women gather
far and wide
a fire is burning
brighter than the sailing sun,
gold embers sparkle
wood crunches
coconuts crack
milk flows toward
a solitary lake
children swing from branches
smiles stretch
like boomerangs
face to face
ear to ear
laughter echoes eternal
the village vibrates
with the sound of union
magnificent drumming
ripples the tide
the night falls
and way up high
the moon is full
it shimmers
on the water.

Meaning in the Suffering

What is suffering?
The corridor to peace
Peace can only be achieved
In the aching hour
In the gallant journey
In the exile of hate.
By the embrace of change
Our hearts bleed
That's what they do
They beat in the chest of an orphan
They loop like a lucid nightmare
They sing like birds
Shatter like skulls
Dance like death.

The mistakes I endured
The friends I lost
The wisdom I gained
Humanity can only be described
As a soup of oppression
Layers upon layers of human suffering
Guiding us toward an unresponsive light
A light that promises hope
A ribbon with which
We trace our dreams.

Suffering, oh suffering!
You are my one true friend.
As I ponder your painful clench
I see the gains
Amid your stench.

Hometown Visitation

Thoughts and feelings
Re-emerge
Like the ruins of a forgotten
Pier.
Hometown, visitation
Where I first began.
Time will pass
The waves will crash
A hurricane heralds the news.
The twinkling cluster
Of Chinese bells drift
In the noble night.
The final days
Of a perfect year
Familiar struggles
In pain and in lesson
I found myself
In a broken mirror
I found your soul
In a photograph.

Remember, don't forget
Be the thing you are
Accept your loved ones
And love the gaps
You aim to fill.
Divinely, I devour,
The peace that never
Stays.
Conflicted, in harmony
My bones are kind.
Nobody
Wants to die,
So they punish you
To stay alive.
I'm thirsty for love
So I seem insane,
Until you finally
See me.

Bethnal Green

Birds circling beneath daylight-levity,
Trains prowling across reverie-mire,
Green dimples covering ocean-feet,
Desperate thumbs plugging pecuniary-beach,
Mind enveloped in cathartic-numb,
Arresting joy through collective-embrace,
Closing door on lonesome skittle,
Soaking bones in marrow-love,
Absent shadow, lurking over curious-dreams,
Youth swinging like pendulum-fate,
Mothers waning before future-clouds,
Naked trees, yearn leaf-guise,
Cranes stitched to skyline-progress,
Dolphins held captive; hearts' opaque-lake.
Beady eyes bound to east-bench,
Success tickling strident pen-sweats.

Burst imagination-pimple,
Notions dribble, heaven-effusions,
Hunger rumbling before success-soup,
Ancient blades, severing family-tie,
Crawling across galaxy-knees,
Whip basement folly, discourse-immune,
Tongue pigeon, startling mind-sparrow,
Colour aligned through finger-searcher,
Idolize art-canvas-money-brew,
Jangles leaking through pocket-kin,
Spirit suffering by self's-hand,
Glove warm under auspices-vice,
Clarity spilling on pallet-creation,
Hogging attention deficit-order,
Forever, I endeavour, love-love,
Ink signing: spirits'-serenity.

Paris Poem

I'm falling in love,
With no one,
Hiding on the edge of shadows.
Voices warm my pillows,
Like pigeons pecking velcro,
Possessed by a wider opening,
I wake up dreaming of memories,
Cos youth will never die.
And in that perched rebuttal,
Your gold is my disguise,
Like blood beneath the river,
We all need someplace to go.
A place to fill our lovely hearts
A place where people feel me,
That's where I belong,
In the skies of loving eyes.

Kunstlers

Life of an artist:
A life dedicated to self-obsession
Self-aggrandisement
Self-exploration
To voyage with the self
To accept the self.
Gee, what a narcissistic mode of being,
But where would we be without it?
No record of the wonderment
Of human civilisation,
That's where.

Enter the Labyrinth

I was cut
from
my Mother's womb
clustered
in a scream
when Mummy left my Daddy
I was far too young to see,
there you'll find
the puzzle
still inside the box
the receipt
is always lost
and it's me
who brunts
the cost.

I'm 33 years old
still, I can't deduce
my mystifying story
my lineage of truth;
first few forward footsteps

living on the run
everything was easy;
the Prodigal Son.

Hitherto,
dear friends
find comfort
in the chaos
disquiet
is my essence
so spare me
from the bliss
choking
in accord
Mummy's
umbilical
cord

Now I wield
a sword
guided by
The Lord.

Sehnsucht

Berlin,
A sanctuary for lost souls.
A dirty, despotic, dream.
A widening vacuum,
Glowing beneath the ashes,
Turning in pain,
Frozen by guilt.
A nibbled nipple,
A smacked arse,
A filthy paradise,
A wounded cat,
Starved of affection,
Moist from the downpour,
And yet still purring
At the prospect of a chin stroke.
Beneath the hipster exteriors
And the pseudo scenes
And false pretenders
Keen to be seen in a scene,
I could see a red ruby,
Reduced to fragments
Scattered across a train track
Revealed by passing trains
That creek and murmur
Bygone duels.

The romance of the bars,
The taste of warm beer,
In cold glass,
The looming smoke
That tickles the rim of your nostril

A drunk, chewing his scabs,
Sucking blood from his knuckle,
In bed with his madness,
Betrayed by sanity,
Enjoying the taste
Of his unborn misery.

I'll never forget,
The cold nights in candlelight,
The threesomes in morning light,
The blackouts in drug pits,
The cracked lips,
The rats,
The slurred chats,
The unhatched panic attacks,
The crisp slurs of hate,
The looping bass,
The chemical tastes,
The strobing face,
The thoughtful thinking
The endless drinking,
The community minds
And stern behinds,
The trust in each other
Free from our mothers!

Berlin, you and I,
We are both orphans of the night
Beckoning new ships of lost souls
Ready to rejoice
A new dawn of
Sweet, sweet, nichts...

Free Association

Emerald eyes
Hungry trees
Reality tunnel
Wheels of spring
Green collision
Nature cries
Purest minds
Birds bequeath
Brazen bee
Kindred colour
Prodromal war
Punching air
Under-ground
Monster missile
Roman shield
Holy ghost
Strawberry hill

Moribund bone
Mellifluous smile
Transient beauty
Falling fruit
Amber thread
Swollen gold
Biker sweat
Bleeding gums
Painted leash
London leather
Berlin baby
Apathy anomie
Shrieking time
Stolen kiss
Joy within
Brain of pain
Flag of art
Art in heart
Back to start.

Floating in Space

a clock face
a star
a trail
a taste
a smell
a fear
a moment
in childhood.

Yesterday's Tomorrow

The greens and the colours
of life's garden lovers,
are pure and ashore through smiles.
Gentile and fearless, the Earth's sun
will heal us; her radiance will live on for miles.

Her heart, always dancing, sand-kingdom
of passing, as the tips of my island taste gold.
Both speaking through silence,
with the passion of violence,
entwined we will never grow old.

But the treason of time is seldom to hide,
if our spirit is invariably waiting.
Amidst our daydream tent,
bones locked like an instrument,
we make love 'til no-ones left hating.

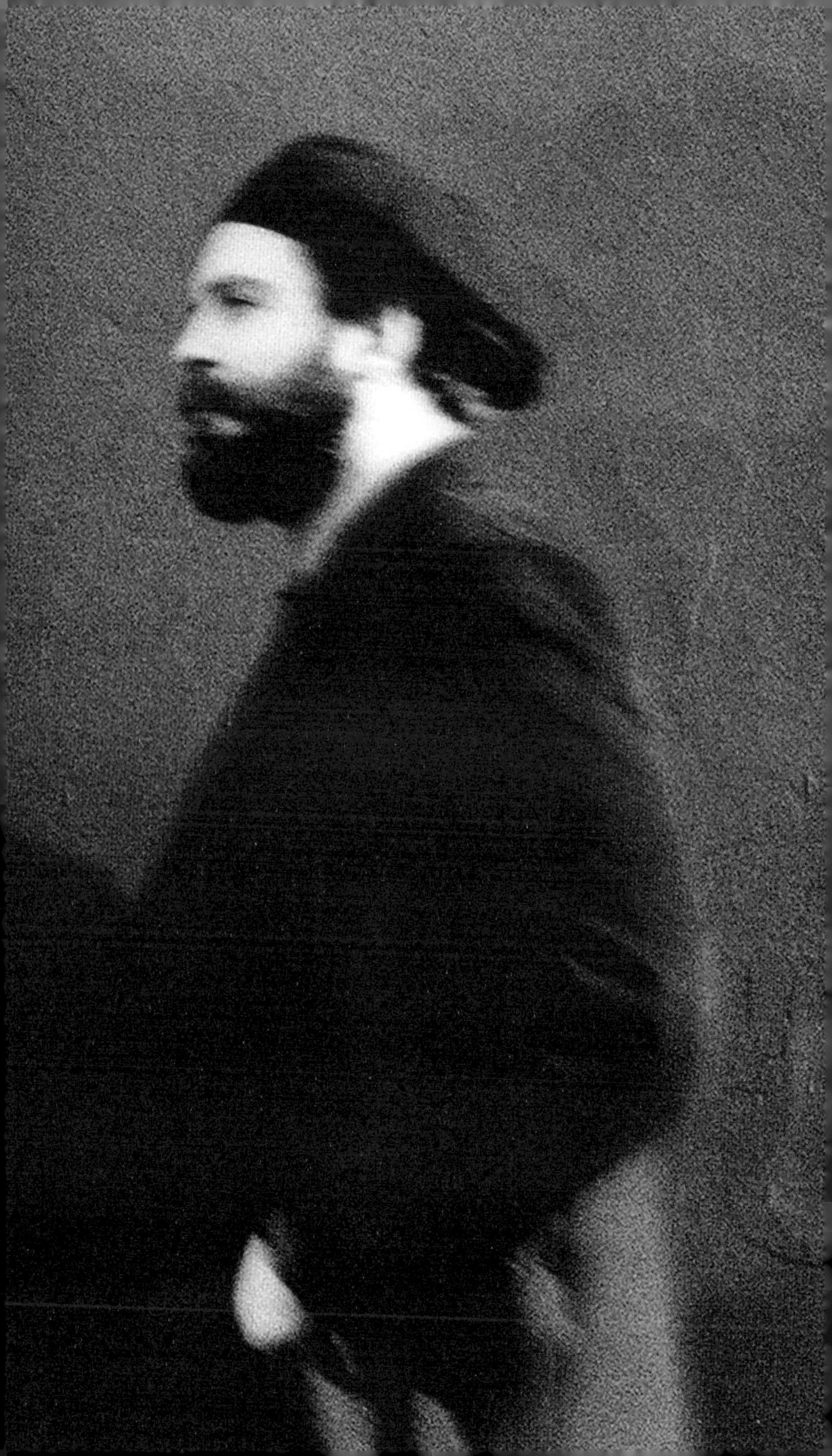

Beyond the sound of hollow horns

Here is a slice, of humble proof:
If all man's words were hung aloof,
Stretched across the hanging gardens,
They'd fasten our attention and beg for our pardons.

But, once the words... crease and dry,
Faith will hasten to spill from the eye,
Leaving the heir with no tangible token,
No truth, no lesson, no ameliorating potion.

Actions are the mighty brute!
For you cannot learn 'til you've felt the boot,
Crack against your wildest plans,
Shatter your ego and bewilder your hands.

Roads are forged in the dauntless journey,
Seldom procured in the preparatory,
So take the step that will murder your words,
As the machinery of night gathers its birds,
Hanging above your every endeavour,
They'll guide the way as long as you surrender,
To life as a movement, not a stagnant sound,
Prove your platitudes, and make yourself proud.

Cry Little Sister

When you're feeling blue
Appreciate all of the beauty
Around you,
The sun will rise again.

Keep the Faith

Sickened by the cynic,
Whose mind is halted by brick.
Blinded by a chasm of darkness,
The partisan reaches for the switch.
Spouting venom in the dark,
The maelstrom, his farthest range.
The switch is flicked,
The light cascades,
and so...
The cynic gives way for change.

George Floyd

The space between
The thuds in his heart
Were filled with pleas
For his Momma.

The Spirit

Before us the pleasures and pains are alive,
Yet the ocean of truth & mystery, coincide.
The crust of one's madness can easily break,
When you believe in a genuine fake.
Devoid of meaning, I refuse to believe,
Beauty in tears or an Autumn leaf.
We mustn't lose faith, lose hope, control,
As you and I are blessed with a soul.
So our purpose is clear, to learn and grow,
Nourish one another,
Like a stream's gracious flow.
And so, the answers may stifle the drive to be,
But let us preserve the unknown,
The fabric of a complex anomaly.

Elsker

under the sheets
you'll find love,
like freckles on
a fading face,
when the bed
bounces
brutishly
it happens again
allied with
the melody
of midnight.

Radici

When I go to the field. If I touch an olive tree.
I think, that this olive tree, is the same olive tree
that has seen my father, my grandfather, even
before my grandfather...

And I think that it's very important that,
every person has good radici (roots)

Roots are not just found beneath the trees and
plants you find in the field, but you have them too.

Your roots are what help you to get on in your life.
Even if a strong wind hits you, though it may throw
you down, break you, if you have strong roots
– and your family roots are the strongest –
perhaps there is no wind that can take you
away from where you are.

Radici

Quando vado nel mio campo e tocco un ulivo,
penso che questo ulivo è lo stesso ulivo
che ha visto mio padre, mio nonno,
e prima ancora mio bisnonno...

E penso anche che sia molto importante
per ogni persona avere buone radici,
come le piante.

Le radici non sono solo quelle sotto
le piante e gli alberi che hai nel tuo campo,
ma le hai anche tu.

Le tue radici sono ciò che ti aiuta ad andare
avanti nella vita. Anche se nella vita accade
che un forte vento contrario ti colpisca, ti
butti giù e ti spezzi, se tu hai forti radici
- e le tue radici familiari sono le piu forti -
forse non esiste vento che possa portarti
via da dove sei.

The open window

under
the sunlight
you're a name
a clink of appointed
syllables
an image
a vibration
chiming inside
another mind
like the
gentle
grind of
the neighbour’s
plates
at supper-time.

November in your soul

alone
in the dark

internal
landscape
draped
in glass

protect
your
flower.

The church bell rings

The church bell rings
Gathers heroic pace
The townspeople wake
From a long cold dream
Torches ignite
Babies find their mothers
The wind howls hard
The rain pours louder
Large gates open
Villagers swarm together
Shuffle in the dark
Owls glare and grumble
A man with a topper
Beckons with a finger
A ‘psst’ and a wink
‘Follow me to the church’

At his highness' request
They followed
With his order
Huddled down the path
Between the falling bricks
They reach
A thunderstorm
A long lightning bolt
Opens up the sky
The onlookers cry.
As tears stream down
The unrelenting rain
The man with the topper
Folds into a dove,
The dove hovers high
Climbing with the bell
He nestles on the spire:
'His truth is marching on!'

Kiss my Dada Lips

Precious Lord,
Cut me loose,
Above the clouds,
So I can plunge,
Into the blue.

Precious Lord,
Hoist me quick,
So I can see,
The world that winds,
Behind the walls,
That I have built.

Precious Lord,
Bowl me down,
Ancient pyramids,
Bury my laughter
In sullen sand,
Quilt my cries
& hold my hand.

Precious Lord!
Erode the eyes
I wore,
When I was blind.

Precious Lord,
Deliver me,
Quick!
From boredom's grip!
Fold me in music,
Unravel the string,
That sits between
The now
& the always.

Precious Lord,
In return,
I vow to never
Return with a frown.

About the sky

unquenched desires
stammered over space
infinitely beautiful
unreasonably sad
heavy as a memory
with the weight of a glance
as long as you're
alive
you're given
a chance.

Bildnis einer Trinkerin

I arrived in København
It was cold and
Nordic,
The air was clear
The evening had fallen
I bought a kebab
To treat myself
Beyond the tumultuous journey
I sat outside
And pressed my behind
On the wet chair
You could feel
The cold structure
Latch like a seatbelt
I ate alone
As young women
With blue eyes
Soft skin

And long ponytails
Plodded along
On big bicycles

No sirens
No seagulls
No fear
No expectations
No joy
No misery,
Balance.

Just me
And my purchase
What lay ahead
Nobody knew
All I knew
Was this kebab
Tasted good
And I was free.

Untitled ii

Dear Minerva,
Thank you for your teaching
You enrich me in order
The gleam of your smile
Echoes in my rib cage
From the well of my heart
The wind still blows
Like the seduction of a string
Like the warmth of your grip
Like the frontiers of hope
Inviting and warm.
Like a child sucking wonder
From a life of abundance
You keep me safe &
I am never alone.

Inchoate

the earth shakes
pegs that grip
our belief system on a thin
string
subsidized by a company
of margins and balance sheets
we emerge in rouge
like lipstick on a hanky
like a fan being spanked
by her idol
we will unite
and in the bright burning sun
we venture
to assimilate
the ambrosia of ideals
endlessly cumming
to the final analysis.

Daydreams in December

As I lay upon the grass
The bluest sky is here to last
Sounds of joy open wide
Birds above hang and glide
Love to be, inside the day
Hope forever; nature stay.

'In the beauty of the lilies
Christ was born across the sea
With a glory in his bosom
that transfigures you and me.
As he died to make men holy
let us die to make men free
'His truth is marching on.'

'Battle Hymn of the Republic'
Song by Odetta

I dedicate this book
to the wonderful teachings of:

Anaïs Nin, Henry Miller, Arthur Rimbaud,
Albert Camus, Francis Coppola,
Jordan Peterson, Mickey Rourke,
Marlon Brando, Jean-Paul Sartre,
Charles Bukowski, Allen Ginsberg,
R. W. Fassbinder, Robert Towne,
John Updike, W. H. Auden, Leonard Cohen,
Cicero, Homer, S. E. Hinton, Muhammad Ali,
Fyodor Dostoyevsky, Carl Jung, Franz Kafka,
Michael Jackson, Martin Amis,
Rainer Maria Rilke, Gil Scott Heron,
Saul Bellow, John Steinbeck, Egar Allen Poe,
Shakespeare & my Mother.

There are times when I lost my confidence,
but I never lost my determination.

Thank you for reading,

Love & truthfully,
Browzan

POIESIS
PUBLISHERS
ποίησις

the activity in which a person brings something into being that did not exist before

ISBN 978-1-5272-9638-1

9 781527 296381